DIARY 2015

PERSONAL INFORMATION

NAME	
ADDRESS	
E-MAIL	
PHONE	
MOBILE	

2 0 1 5

January

Su	Mo	Tu	We	Th	Fr	Sa
				1	2	3
4	5	6	7	8	9	10
11	12	13	14	15	16	17
18	19	20	21	22	23	24
25	26	27	28	29	30	31

February

Su	Mo	Tu	We	Th	Fr	Sa
1	2	3	4	5	6	7
8	9	10	11	12	13	14
15	16	17	18	19	20	21
22	23	24	25	26	27	28

March

Su	Mo	Tu	We	Th	Fr	Sa
1	2	3	4	5	6	7
8	9	10	11	12	13	14
15	16	17	18	19	20	21
22	23	24	25	26	27	28
29	30	31				

April

Su	Mo	Tu	We	Th	Fr	Sa
			1	2	3	4
5	6	7	8	9	10	11
12	13	14	15	16	17	18
19	20	21	22	23	24	25
26	27	28	29	30		

May

Su	Mo	Tu	We	Th	Fr	Sa
31					1	2
3	4	5	6	7	8	9
10	11	12	13	14	15	16
17	18	19	20	21	22	23
24	25	26	27	28	29	30

June

Su	Mo	Tu	We	Th	Fr	Sa
	1	2	3	4	5	6
7	8	9	10	11	12	13
14	15	16	17	18	19	20
21	22	23	24	25	26	27
28	29	30				

July

Su	Mo	Tu	We	Th	Fr	Sa
			1	2	3	4
5	6	7	8	9	10	11
12	13	14	15	16	17	18
19	20	21	22	23	24	25
26	27	28	29	30	31	

August

Su	Mo	Tu	We	Th	Fr	Sa
30	31					1
2	3	4	5	6	7	8
9	10	11	12	13	14	15
16	17	18	19	20	21	22
23	24	25	26	27	28	29

September

Su	Mo	Tu	We	Th	Fr	Sa
		1	2	3	4	5
6	7	8	9	10	11	12
13	14	15	16	17	18	19
20	21	22	23	24	25	26
27	28	29	30			

October

Su	Mo	Tu	We	Th	Fr	Sa
				1	2	3
4	5	6	7	8	9	10
11	12	13	14	15	16	17
18	19	20	21	22	23	24
25	26	27	28	29	30	31

November

Su	Mo	Tu	We	Th	Fr	Sa
1	2	3	4	5	6	7
8	9	10	11	12	13	14
15	16	17	18	19	20	21
22	23	24	25	26	27	28
29	30					

December

Su	Mo	Tu	We	Th	Fr	Sa
		1	2	3	4	5
6	7	8	9	10	11	12
13	14	15	16	17	18	19
20	21	22	23	24	25	26
27	28	29	30	31		

my special dates

2016

January

Su	Mo	Tu	We	Th	Fr	Sa
					1	2
3	4	5	6	7	8	9
10	11	12	13	14	15	16
17	18	19	20	21	22	23
24	25	26	27	28	29	30
31						

February

Su	Mo	Tu	We	Th	Fr	Sa
1	2	3	4	5	6	
7	8	9	10	11	12	13
14	15	16	17	18	19	20
21	22	23	24	25	26	27
28	29					

March

Su	Mo	Tu	We	Th	Fr	Sa
		1	2	3	4	5
6	7	8	9	10	11	12
13	14	15	16	17	18	19
20	21	22	23	24	25	26
27	28	29	30	31		

April

Su	Mo	Tu	We	Th	Fr	Sa
					1	2
3	4	5	6	7	8	9
10	11	12	13	14	15	16
17	18	19	20	21	22	23
24	25	26	27	28	29	30

May

Su	Mo	Tu	We	Th	Fr	Sa
1	2	3	4	5	6	7
8	9	10	11	12	13	14
15	16	17	18	19	20	21
22	23	24	25	26	27	28
29	30	31				

June

Su	Mo	Tu	We	Th	Fr	Sa
			1	2	3	4
5	6	7	8	9	10	11
12	13	14	15	16	17	18
19	20	21	22	23	24	25
26	27	28	29	30		

July

Su	Mo	Tu	We	Th	Fr	Sa
					1	2
3	4	5	6	7	8	9
10	11	12	13	14	15	16
17	18	19	20	21	22	23
24	25	26	27	28	29	30
31						

August

Su	Mo	Tu	We	Th	Fr	Sa
	1	2	3	4	5	6
7	8	9	10	11	12	13
14	15	16	17	18	19	20
21	22	23	24	25	26	27
28	29	30	31			

September

Su	Mo	Tu	We	Th	Fr	Sa
				1	2	3
4	5	6	7	8	9	10
11	12	13	14	15	16	17
18	19	20	21	22	23	24
25	26	27	28	29	30	

October

Su	Mo	Tu	We	Th	Fr	Sa
						1
2	3	4	5	6	7	8
9	10	11	12	13	14	15
16	17	18	19	20	21	22
23	24	25	26	27	28	29
30	31					

November

Su	Mo	Tu	We	Th	Fr	Sa
		1	2	3	4	5
6	7	8	9	10	11	12
13	14	15	16	17	18	19
20	21	22	23	24	25	26
27	28	29	30			

December

Su	Mo	Tu	We	Th	Fr	Sa
				1	2	3
4	5	6	7	8	9	10
11	12	13	14	15	16	17
18	19	20	21	22	23	24
25	26	27	28	29	30	31

my special dates

January 2015

New Year's Day
Thursday
1

Friday
2

Saturday
3

Sunday
4

January 2015

Monday
5

Tuesday
6

Wednesday
7

Thursday
8

Friday
9

Saturday
10

Sunday
11

Monday
12

Tuesday
13

Wednesday
14

Thursday **15**
Friday **16**
Saturday **17**
Sunday **18**

January 2015

Monday
19

Tuesday
20

Wednesday
21

Thursday
22

Friday
23

Saturday
24

Sunday
25

January 2015

Monday
26

Tuesday
27

Wednesday
28

Thursday
29

Friday
30

Saturday
31

February 2015
Sunday
1

February 2015

Monday
2

Tuesday
3

Wednesday
4

Thursday
5

Friday
6

Saturday
7

Sunday
8

February 2015

Monday
9

Tuesday
10

Wednesday
11

Thursday
12

Friday
13

Saturday
14

Sunday
15

February 2015

Monday
16

Tuesday
17

Wednesday
18

Thursday
19

Friday
20

Saturday
21

Sunday
22

February 2015

Monday
23

Tuesday
24

Wednesday
25

Thursday **26**
Friday **27**
Saturday **28**
March 2015 Sunday **1**

March 2015

Monday
2

Tuesday
3

Wednesday
4

Thursday
5

Friday
6

Saturday
7

Sunday
8

March 2015

Monday

9

Tuesday

10

Wednesday

11

Thursday
12

Friday
13

Saturday
14

Sunday
15

March 2015

Monday
16

Tuesday
17

Wednesday
18

Thursday **19**
Friday **20**
Saturday **21**
Sunday **22**

March 2015

Monday
23

Tuesday
24

Wednesday
25

Thursday
26

Friday
27

Saturday
28

Sunday
29

Monday
30

Tuesday
31

April 2015
Wednesday
1

Thursday
2

Good Friday
Friday
3

Saturday
4

Easter Sunday
Sunday
5

April 2015

Monday	Easter
Monday	
6	

Tuesday

7

Wednesday

8

Thursday
9

Friday
10

Saturday
11

Sunday
12

April 2015

Monday
13

Tuesday
14

Wednesday
15

Thursday
16

Friday
17

Saturday
18

Sunday
19

April 2015

Monday
20

Tuesday
21

Wednesday
22

Thursday
23

Friday
24

Saturday
25

Sunday
26

Monday
27

Tuesday
28

Wednesday
29

Thursday
30

May 2015
Friday
1

Saturday
2

Sunday
3

May 2015

Monday Holiday **4**	Early May Bank
Tuesday **5**	
Wednesday **6**	

Thursday
7

Friday
8

Saturday
9

Sunday
10

May 2015

Monday
11

Tuesday
12

Wednesday
13

Thursday
14

Friday
15

Saturday
16

Sunday
17

May 2015

Monday
18

Tuesday
19

Wednesday
20

Thursday
21

Friday
22

Saturday
23

Sunday
24

May 2015

Monday Holiday **25**	Spring Bank
Tuesday **26**	
Wednesday **27**	

| Thursday |
| 28 |

| Friday |
| 29 |

| Saturday |
| 30 |

| Sunday |
| 31 |

June 2015

Monday

1

Tuesday

2

Wednesday

3

Thursday
4

Friday
5

Saturday
6

Sunday
7

June 2015

Monday
8

Tuesday
9

Wednesday
10

Thursday
11

Friday
12

Saturday
13

Sunday
14

June 2015

Monday
15

Tuesday
16

Wednesday
17

Thursday
18

Friday
19

Saturday
20

Sunday
21

Monday
22

Tuesday
23

Wednesday
24

Thursday
25

Friday
26

Saturday
27

Sunday
28

June 2015

Monday
29

Tuesday
30

July 2015
Wednesday
1

Thursday
2

Friday
3

Saturday
4

Sunday
5

July 2015

Monday
6

Tuesday
7

Wednesday
8

Thursday
9

Friday
10

Saturday
11

Sunday
12

Monday
13

Tuesday
14

Wednesday
15

Thursday
16

Friday
17

Saturday
18

Sunday
19

July 2015

Monday
20

Tuesday
21

Wednesday
22

Thursday
23

Friday
24

Saturday
25

Sunday
26

July 2015

Monday
27

Tuesday
28

Wednesday
29

Thursday
30

Friday
31

August 2015
Saturday
1

Sunday
2

August 2015

Monday
3

Tuesday
4

Wednesday
5

Thursday
6

Friday
7

Saturday
8

Sunday
9

August 2015

Monday

10

Tuesday

11

Wednesday

12

Thursday
13

Friday
14

Saturday
15

Sunday
16

August 2015

Monday
17

Tuesday
18

Wednesday
19

Thursday
20

Friday
21

Saturday
22

Sunday
23

August 2015

Monday
24

Tuesday
25

Wednesday
26

Thursday
27

Friday
28

Saturday
29

Sunday
30

August 2015

Monday   Summer Bank Holiday
31

September 2015

Tuesday
1

Wednesday
2

Thursday
3

Friday
4

Saturday
5

Sunday
6

September 2015

Monday
7

Tuesday
8

Wednesday
9

Thursday
10

Friday
11

Saturday
12

Sunday
13

September 2015

Monday
14

Tuesday
15

Wednesday
16

Thursday
17

Friday
18

Saturday
19

Sunday
20

September 2015

Monday
21

Tuesday
22

Wednesday
23

September 2015

Thursday
24

Friday
25

Saturday
26

Sunday
27

82

September 2015

Monday
28

Tuesday
29

Wednesday
30

Thursday
1

Friday
2

Saturday
3

Sunday
4

October 2015

Monday
5

Tuesday
6

Wednesday
7

Thursday
8

Friday
9

Saturday
10

Sunday
11

October 2015

Monday
12

Tuesday
13

Wednesday
14

Thursday
15

Friday
16

Saturday
17

Sunday
18

October 2015

Monday
19

Tuesday
20

Wednesday
21

Thursday
22

Friday
23

Saturday
24

Sunday
25

Monday
26

Tuesday
27

Wednesday
28

Thursday
29

Friday
30

Saturday
31

November 2015
Sunday
1

November 2015

Monday
2

Tuesday
3

Wednesday
4

Thursday
5

Friday
6

Saturday
7

Sunday
8

November 2015

Monday
9

Tuesday
10

Wednesday
11

Thursday
12

Friday
13

Saturday
14

Sunday
15

November 2015

Monday
16

Tuesday
17

Wednesday
18

Thursday
19

Friday
20

Saturday
21

Sunday
22

November 2015

Monday
23

Tuesday
24

Wednesday
25

Thursday
26

Friday
27

Saturday
28

Sunday
29

November 2015

Monday

30

December 2015

Tuesday

1

Wednesday

2

Thursday
3

Friday
4

Saturday
5

Sunday
6

December 2015

Monday
7

Tuesday
8

Wednesday
9

Thursday
10

Friday
11

Saturday
12

Sunday
13

December 2015

Monday
14

Tuesday
15

Wednesday
16

Thursday
17

Friday
18

Saturday
19

Sunday
20

December 2015

Monday
21

Tuesday
22

Wednesday
23

Thursday
24

Christmas Day
Friday
25

Saturday
26

Sunday
27

December 2015

Monday	Boxing Day Holiday
28	

Tuesday

29

Wednesday

30

December 2015

Thursday
31

January 2016
New Year's Day
Friday
1

Saturday
2

Sunday
3

January 2016

Monday
4

Tuesday
5

Wednesday
6

MY NOTE BOOK

MY CONTACTS

NAME	MOBILE	EMAIL

NAME	MOBILE	EMAIL

MY FAVORITE INTERNET SITES

WWW	URL	DATE

MY PROJECTS

www.ingramcontent.com/pod-product-compliance
Lightning Source LLC
Chambersburg PA
CBHW020917180526
45163CB00007B/2779